The Planets

Your Mission to Saturn

by M. J. Cosson
illustrated by Scott Burroughs

Content Consultant
Diane M. Bollen, Research Scientist,
Cornell University

magic wagon

visit us at www.abdopublishing.com

Printed in the United States of America, North Mankato, Minnesota.
052011
092011

 THIS BOOK CONTAINS AT LEAST 10% RECYCLED MATERIALS.

Text by M. J. Cosson
Illustrations by Scott Burroughs
Edited by Holly Saari
Series design and cover production by Becky Daum
Interior production by Christa Schneider

Library of Congress Cataloging-in-Publication Data
Cosson, M. J.
  Your mission to Saturn / by M.J. Cosson ; illustrated by Scott Burroughs.
     p. cm. — (The planets)
  Includes index.
  ISBN 978-1-61641-682-9
  1. Saturn (Planet)—Juvenile literature. I. Burroughs, Scott, ill. II. Title.
  QB671.C67 2012
  523.46—dc22
                              2011006778

Table of Contents

Imagine You Could Go

Saturn is the fancy planet. It is all dressed up with the most beautiful rings. It would be fun to visit Saturn, but no one has ever been there. You can only imagine what it would be like.

You can see Saturn from Earth without using a telescope. It looks like a bright yellow star. But you have to use a telescope to see its rings.

Distance from Earth

You have a powerful spaceship lined up for your trip. And you're going to need it to get to Saturn. It is the sixth planet from the sun. You'll need to travel more than 740 million miles (1.2 billion km) away from Earth.

You climb into your spaceship. Once you're settled in, you read some about Saturn. The planet is mostly a big ball of gas. It is the second-largest planet in the solar system. You could put about ten Earths inside Saturn!

Saturn's Rings

Months later, you look out the window. You start seeing chunks of ice and rock. Some are the size of pebbles. Others are as large as houses. You know where you are. You're traveling through Saturn's rings!

MOONS

- ☒ Aegaeon
- ☐ Daphnis
- ☒ Dione
- ☐ Greip
- ☒ Hati
- ☒ Pan
- ☐ Rhea
- Skoll
- ...vos
- Titan

Moons

You start to see some of the many moons of Saturn. Some are between the rings. You can name the moons. You spot Aegaeon and Greip. There's Dione and Pan. You wish you had time to find all the moons. There are at least 62!

The first moon you visit is Enceladus. The ice on its surface makes it one of the brightest objects in the night sky. Enceladus is so shiny that it reflects almost all of the sunlight that hits it. It is so cold that you don't stay long.

The temperature on Enceladus is about –330 degrees Fahrenheit (–201°C). If you didn't have your special suit on, you would freeze instantly.

Next, you visit Saturn's biggest moon, Titan. It is even bigger than the planet Mercury. Something about Titan reminds you a little bit of Earth.

Now you see why! Titan has many of the same features that Earth has. It has clouds with rain and snow. It has mountains, lakes, and rivers. The liquid isn't water, though. It's a mixture of ethane and methane.

Gases

You zoom over to Saturn. Beneath the clouds are gases including helium and hydrogen.

Saturn is the least dense of all the planets. If you could do a floating experiment with a piece of Saturn and a piece of Earth, the piece of Earth would sink. It is heavier than water. The piece of Saturn would float. It is lighter than water.

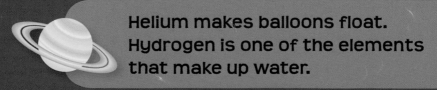

Helium makes balloons float. Hydrogen is one of the elements that make up water.

Liquid Layer

Saturn's gravity is pulling you down below its atmosphere. The gravity is just a little stronger on Saturn than on Earth.

Now you've reached the wet part of Saturn. You've prepared for this by putting on your scuba gear. You're in a liquid ocean of hydrogen and helium.

Core

You're really excited about what's coming next. Are you about to make an amazing discovery? Scientists think the core of this giant gas ball is probably solid. It is likely made of rock. You get to see if it's true and bring your answer back to Earth.

Saturn is very far from the sun, so the outside is very cold. But the inner part of Saturn is hot.

Years

You leave the core behind and look out to the sky. The sun is very far away. You think about living on Saturn for a year. How long would that be in Earth time? Almost 30 years! That's how long it takes for Saturn to orbit the sun one time.

Saturn tilts like Earth does. So it has four seasons, just like Earth. But each season on Saturn is more than seven years long!

Days

You watch the sun slide out of view behind Saturn. Is it getting dark already? You haven't been here very long. What happened?

Saturn spins around like a top, just like Earth does. The time it takes for a planet to spin around once is one day. This is the time from one sunrise to the next. On Earth, one day is 24 hours. On Saturn, one day is ten-and-a-half hours. That explains it!

Saturn spins so fast that it seems to bulge at the equator. It looks like a long skirt that flares out when someone twirls. Jupiter is the only planet that spins faster than Saturn.

Storms

You notice a storm in the distance and you take a closer look. You think it might be what scientists call the Great White Spot. This is the stormy area that looks white through telescopes on Earth.

You try to get close, but you can't. Your instruments tell you the winds are blowing more than 1,000 miles per hour (1,609 km/h). That is about as fast as a bullet traveling out of a gun.

Time for Sleep

You've had a great time on Saturn. But these storms make you wish for your nice warm bed. It's time to stop pretending and get to sleep. Perhaps you will visit Saturn in your dreams, too.

29

How Do Scientists Know about Saturn?

Saturn can be seen without a telescope, so people have known about it since long ago. In 1610, Galileo looked at Saturn through a telescope. He thought he saw arms on the planet.

In 1659, Christiaan Huygens looked at Saturn with a better telescope. He saw that the "arms" were actually rings. He also discovered Saturn's largest moon, Titan. In the 1800s, James Keeler found out that Saturn's rings are made of particles.

In 1973, the National Aeronautics and Space Administration (NASA) launched *Pioneer 11*. This was the first spacecraft to explore Saturn. It flew by Saturn for the first time in 1979. It gathered information about Saturn's atmosphere. It found another ring and another moon.

Cassini was launched in 1997. After flying by Venus and Jupiter, it reached Saturn in July 2004. It was the first spacecraft to orbit Saturn. In January 2005, *Cassini* dropped a vehicle to the surface of Titan. The vehicle took many pictures of Titan and sent back new information about Saturn's largest moon. As of 2011, *Cassini* is still orbiting Saturn.

Saturn Facts

Position: Sixth planet from sun

Distance from sun: Average of 886 million miles (1.4 billion km)

Diameter (distance through the planet's middle): 74,900 miles (120,540 km)

Length of orbit (year): About 29.5 Earth years

Length of rotation (day): About 10.5 hours

Gravity: Slightly stronger than Earth's gravity

Number of moons: At least 62

Main moons: Mimas, Enceladus, Tethys, Dione, Rhea, Titan, Hyperion

Words to Know

atmosphere—the layer of gases surrounding a planet.

core—the center of a planet.

dense—made of material that is tightly packed together.

equator—an imaginary line around the center of a planet.

gas—a substance that spreads out to fit what it is in, like air in a tire.

gravity—the force that pulls a smaller object toward a larger object.

orbit—to travel around something, usually in an oval path.

solar system—a star and the objects, such as planets, that travel around it.

Learn More

Books

Allyn, Daisy. *Saturn: The Ringed Planet*. New York: Gareth Stevens, 2007.

Gibbons, Gail. *The Planets*. New York: Holiday House, 2007.

Goldsmith, Mike. *Solar System*. London: Kingfisher, 2010.

Web Sites

To learn more about Saturn, visit ABDO Group online at **www.abdopublishing.com**. Web sites about Saturn are featured on our Book Links page. These links are routinely monitored and updated to provide the most current information available.

Index